The XXL BBQ Cookbook

The Complete Grilling Guide - Quick and Delicious Recipes for a perfect Barbecue Season incl. Side Dishes, Dips and Desserts

James Hammond

ISBN- 9798503781823

TABLE OF CONTENTS

INTRODUCTION

What is barbecue cooking?

Barbecue cooking, also known as BBQ in the UK and other countries, used fire and smoke to cook food. A variety of foods can be infused with rich and delicious flavours as they are smoked over charcoal, wood or gas-fired grills.

Many BBQ dishes have an American twist to them since BBQ-style cookery is extremely popular in the USA. However, BBQ dishes are popular across the world, with people in Southern hemisphere countries even taking a BBQ grill out onto the beach at Christmas to cook a BBQ style feast.

BBQ flavours have become so popular in the modern age that many companies have produced BBQ flavoured products to meet consumers' desires. Who doesn't love a bag of barbecue flavour crisps?

A Flavoursome History of BBQ

The history of BBQ cooking is a long and exciting one. The modern BBQ as we know it has evolved from ancient practices that transformed into the BBQ style cookery we know and love today.

The word "barbecue" is believed to be derived from an Arawak and Timucua word "barabicu." The Arawak people originated from the Caribbean while the Timucua **people** were a native American tribe found mainly in Florida.

When Spanish explorers landed in the New World in the sixteenth century, these native people's form of BBQ cookery impressed them and they took BBQ back to their homeland. The word "barbecoa" began to be used in the Spanish language as this type of cookery was popularised in Spain.

In its earliest form, BBQ cooking comprised roasting meet over a hole in the ground. It might sound simplistic compared to some of the innovative and high-tech BBQs that are available in the modern age, but the rich and flavoursome food that resulted from it gave rise to increased popularity across the world.

By the seventeenth century, BBQ had made it to English shores and, as they say, the rest is history. Over the past few centuries, BBQ has gone from strength to strength, impressing generations and driving the technology that allows us to chargrill delicious food. In the present day, an array of options is available for BBQ grills, with all kinds of cooking materials available, including coal, gas and wood.

How to Host the Perfect BBQ Party

One of the best things about BBQ food is that it encourages sociable parties for all your friends and family. Of course, when you are the host of a BBQ party you want your guests to feel welcome, enjoy an incredible ambience and taste the most delectable foods. So, what are the best ways to ensure that you give your nearest and dearest a remarkably unforgettable experience at your BBQ?

The preparation for your BBQ party begins the night before. It is important to carry out as much pre-preparation as you can. This can include making your dips and cold sides and having burger patties ready to come right out of the fridge and go straight onto the grill when your guests arrive at your gathering. Ensuring that you are ready to go on the day will lessen any stress associated with hosting a party and allow you to enjoy the day without needing to run around like a headless chicken!

Before you host your party, it's also essential to be sure that you are fully stocked up with fuel for your BBQ grill. The last thing that you want to find on the day of your party is that you are low on fuel and will not be able to cook the food. Always keep a backup supply so that you will not run out and leave your guests hungry. As safety is extremely important, keep a fire extinguisher on hand just in case. The chances of needing the fire extinguisher are extremely low but it will give you extra safety and peace of mind to have one nearby/

As important as the quality of the food is, your atmosphere and décor are equally important. Put some thought into planning your party, infusing the gathering with your signature style. Scatter chairs around the garden or patio area where you are hosting the party so that your guests have a comfortable place to rest their legs after hours of mingling with friends. Drape fairy light across small tables or wrap them around your washing line to give the party an ethereal ambience that will be particularly impressive as the sun starts to set below the horizon. You can also add other decoration like balloons and streamers to add another unique dimension to the gathering.

Don't forget the drinks! Provide a range of alcoholic and soft drinks that will suit everyone's tastes. If you enjoy whipping up a cocktail or two, offer your guests a delicious Long Island Ice Tea, Mojito or Cosmopolitan. Not only will you impress them with your grilling skills but your cocktail-making skills will be a big tick in their box. Ensure that you also provide a varied array of soft drinks too so that nobody goes thirsty. If you have younger children at the party, include some drinks that will appeal to them like cordials and fruit juices. As a bonus, drinks will keep your guests happy and satisfied while you are firing up the BBQ and cooking their sumptuous meals.

If there are children at your party, offer some entertainment that will keep them occupied while they wait for their food and after they have finished their meals. Games like Twister or board games are the perfect pastime to stop children from getting bored. You can also add in a little entertainment for the adults too. Trivia quizzes are a great way to keep everyone charmed and engaged whilst also providing the opportunity for everyone to get involved and mingle. If you really want to push the boat out, why not set up a karaoke machine?

When it comes to cooking, it is your time to shine! The recipes in this book will give you the upper hand with providing your guests with unique, modern and deeply flavoursome meals that will have them coming back for second and third helpings. It is really important to cater to all your partygoers' dietary needs. If you have vegetarian and vegan guests, include some options for them on your menu so that they have delicious food to eat and feel included in the gathering.

While BBQ cooking is often associated with savoury meals, sweet foods shine when they are cooked on the BBQ. Bananas, pineapples and apples can be transformed from ordinary fruits into a taste sensation with a simple roasting on the grill. Ensure that you keep a tub of ice cream in the freezer and a carton of cream in the refrigerator so that you have something smooth and creamy to serve with your desserts too.

Of course, whatever else you do during your BBQ party, the most important thing of all is to enjoy it. Whether you are an experienced host or this is your very first time hosting a BBQ, enjoy every moment. Snap as many pictures as you can for posterity so that you can fondly gaze back at the memories of the day. Stay relaxed and welcome every guest so that they can attend the BBQ of their lifetime!

Tips for BBQing

Tip One: Choose the right BBQ

Pick the right BBQ to suit your needs and requirements. Before you buy a BBQ, do some research. Consider the size of the BBQ that will fit in the available space that you have. You may choose a built-in BBQ or a freestanding one that can be put away when it is not in use. What's more, decide on the fuel that is right for you when you are selecting your BBQ. Reflect on factors such as cost-efficiency and eco-friendliness.

Tip Two: Always have a backup supply of fuel

Whatever fuel you choose to cook with, keep an extra supply in your shed or garage so that you do not run out on the day. It is extremely important to be sure that you have sufficient fuel, both to avoid any hiccups and to feel a sense of reassurance that nothing will go wrong.

Tip Three: Regularly clean your BBQ

If you haven't used your BBQ for a while, make sure that you clean it thoroughly before use. There are many handy ways to clean a BBQ. One unique solution to removing old dirt and grease is to rub half an onion over the grill area. Once you have done this, you can remove the excess grime with a piece of paper, damp newspaper or an old cloth. Vinegar and lemon juice also work well for breaking down stubborn grime and then your BBQ can be cleaned with a cloth.

Tip Four: Keep your BBQ covered

When you are not using your BBQ keep the lid down and store it in a dry area if that is possible. While many BBQ grills are resistant to the weather as they are designed for outdoor usage, it can still help to maintain the life of your BBQ if you store it somewhere clean and dry where it will not be vulnerable to any chance of rusting or corrosion.

Tip Five: Opt for routine servicing

Keeping your BBQ in optimum working order will ensure that your equipment has not developed any leaks and is very safe to use. You would not drive your car without getting yearly services for it and the principle works the same way when you are looking after your BBQ

Tip Six: Be sure you have all the right equipment

A workman is only as good as their tools and the same applies to a chef and their BBQ. For BBQing, you may need utensils such as BBQ tongs, a sharp steak knife for carving the meat and skewers for using with your kebabs. Keep a carving board nearby to make it easier to cut through steaks too.

Tip Seven: Put safety first

Keep kids away from the BBQ as much as you can. This can be difficult when you are hosting a party in your garden and there are young children present who want to run around but you can divide off the area where you have the BBQ itself to ensure that no kids get access to it. It is also a good idea to keep a fire extinguisher on hand just in case, although the chances of anything catching alight is very low, especially with modern BBQs.

Tip Eight: Choose the best ingredients

What you put into a BBQ partially determines what you will get out of it. By selecting the freshest ingredients, you will already give yourself an advantage when it comes to the flavour of the food and it can make a noticeable difference. Buy local, organic produce if possible, to give your food the most intense and stunning taste. When you are choosing meats, opt for superior cuts and try to use fresh, rather than frozen products.

Tip Nine: Allow the food to rest

It can be tempting to serve the food immediately as soon as it is off the grill, but when you are cooking meat products, they will benefit from a few minutes of rest. This allows the meat to finish cooking through when it is off the heat and will enhance the ultimate flavour of the cooking. This will give your friends and family a taste experience like they have never known before.

Tip Ten: Present the food beautifully

An integral part of BBQing food is the aesthetics of the finished product. When you cook your food, aim to imbue it with the characteristic grill lines that are associated with BBQ food. This traditional aspect of BBQing will deliver the complete and polished BBQ experience to everyone you are serving with your foods. It gives your BBQ a professional dimension that will be extremely appealing.

The Health Benefits of Using a BBQ Grill

Did you know that BBQ food is not only extremely tasty, but it also offers a variety of health benefits too? Cooking food on a BBQ grill is an extremely good way to keep your consumption of fat lower, it can help you increase your fruit and vegetable intake and it can ensure that you get more nutrients from the foods you eat.

LOWER FAT INTAKE

Cooking food over a BBQ can ensure that your fat intake is lower than with other methods of cooking the food. When you cook steaks or burgers in a pan or the oven, the meat sits in the fat and it does not drip away. However, on a BBQ, the fat drizzles off the surface of the meat ensuring that there is less fat present when you ultimately come to eat the food. What's more, you will also be likely to use less added fat during the cooking process as BBQ food does not require the same quantities of butter or oil as frying or roasting needs. Ultimately this can reduce your overall calorie intake and help you to lose weight and maintain a healthy diet.

INCREASED FRUIT AND VEGETABLE INTAKE

As grilling fruit and veggies on a BBQ grill is so easy, it is a simple way to boost your daily intake of these healthy and nutrient-rich foods. With recipes like vegetable kebabs and easy grilled fruit recipes, you may not even notice that you are eating more fruit and veg than normal when you choose these tasty treats.

RETAIN MORE NUTRIENTS IN YOUR FOOD

BBQ food helps to preserve the vitamin content in certain foods. Studies have shown that riboflavin and thiamine levels are higher when food is grilled on a BBQ than when it is cooked using other methods. Consequently, you will absorb a higher amount of these essential nutrients, promoting overall improved health. Many other methods of cooking sap the nutrients from your food, so if you are looking for a way to ensure that your meals are nutrient-rich, delicious and will help you to maintain your overall health, then BBQing more often is an excellent solution to this.

FRESH AIR AND SUNLIGHT ARE GOOD FOR YOU

BBQs promote spending time outdoors in the fresh air and sunlight. Staying cooped up in a kitchen when you cook or spending too much time inside can prevent you from getting the exercise and UV light that you need. Being out in your garden means that you will likely do more steps in a day which is proven to be good for weight loss, heart health and has many other advantages too. Equally, sunlight is an excellent way to increase your levels of vitamin D, which is important for many functions in the body including healthy teeth and bones and an improved immune system. Kids will benefit in a similar way to adults and everyone can experience the feeling of a better mood that is promoted by time outside.

BBQ PARTIES ARE A SOCIABLE EVENT

You may not realise it, but socialising is good for your psychological and emotional wellbeing. As BBQs are events that tend to be sociable, this can ensure that you benefit from having your loved ones around you and provide you with an opportunity to mingle with friends. Many studies have demonstrated the psychological benefits that can be gained when you socialise with friends and family and BBQs are an excellent way to facilitate this.

What to look for when buying your BBQ

There are many considerations that you should focus on when you are buying your BBQ, whether it is your first one or a replacement for a previous grill. Firstly, consider the fuel source that you want to use.

FUEL TYPE

Would you prefer a charcoal grill or one that runs on gas fuel? Gas BBQs tend to be slightly more expensive than charcoal ones but they are also quicker to fire up and it can be easier to control the temperature when you use a gas BBQ.

YOUR BUDGET

There is a BBQ to suit every budget but, of course, higher-priced equipment tends to offer an increased range of features. More high-spec machines will give you a more sophisticated cooking experience but they are likely to set you back considerably more than entry-level BBQs.

RUNNING COSTS

Gas BBQs, in general, are more expensive to run than charcoal-fuelled BBQs. This means that you may find that your expenditure is higher in the long run if you buy a gas BBQ. However, if you are only buying it for occasional use, the range of features that you will find in gas versions may make them your preference.

TO COVER OR NOT TO COVER?

Purchasing a BBQ that has a cover or a lid can help to preserve the longevity of your equipment, especially if it is stored outside. Covering the grill when it is not in use ensures that the grill plate will not be susceptible to wear due to adverse weather conditions like rain, sleet and snow. What is more, when you are cooking, BBQs with a lid allow you more control over the cooking process and help to control the temperature too.

AVAILABLE SPACE

The size of the BBQ that you purchase will often be determined by the size of your garden or how spacious your storage area is if you wish to put the BBQ away when it is not in use. There are extremely large and impressive models available, as well as more compact BBQs so you will be able to find the ideal BBQ that suits the space you have available in your home.

RECIPES

MAGNIFICENT MAIN COURSES

BBQ food is a taste sensation that is perfect for warm-weather parties. These main courses will have your family and your guests revelling in the gorgeous scents and moreish flavours of perfectly grilled food. So, fire up the grill and give these tasty main courses a try.

BEST BBQ STEAK

For a summer feast, nothing beats a sumptuous steak hot off the BBQ. One of the quintessential BBQ dishes, this steak will leave your mouth watering with its tender meat, succulent flavours and delectable scent.

Time: **15 minutes** | Serves: **4**

INGREDIENTS:

- 4 Sirloin or fillet steaks
- 80 ml soy sauce
- 120 ml olive oil
- 80 ml lemon juice
- 40 ml Worcestershire sauce
- 4 cloves of garlic, minced
- 2 tsp chopped fresh parsley
- ½ tsp black pepper
- Pinch of salt

METHOD:

1. In a bowl, combine the soy sauce, olive oil, lemon juice, Worcestershire sauce, minced garlic, parsley, pepper and salt.

2. Add your steaks to the bowl, ensuring that they are fully covered by the marinade and place them in the refrigerator to sit overnight, ensuring that the meat will soak up all the flavours of the marinade.

3. When you are ready to serve the steaks, remove them from the fridge and allow them to sit for 20 minutes to come up to room temperature.

4. Place the steaks on the BBQ grill and leave them for 1.5 to 5 minutes as they become a golden-brown colour. Cooking time will vary depending on how rare or well-done you want the steaks to be.

5. Turn the steaks and cook for another 1.5 to 5 minutes on the other side and then remove from the grill using tongs.

6. Place on a board and allow the steaks to rest for a few minutes before serving.

PER SERVING:

Calories: 290 | Carbs: 35 g | Fat: 11 g | Protein: 6 g

MEXICAN BEEF BRISKET

A spicy beef brisket grilled on your BBQ; this dish is perfect for anyone who is looking for a unique twist to their BBQ food. This recipe uses a combination of slow cooking and BBQing to maximise the ultimate taste sensation.

Time: **30 minutes** | Serves: **4**

INGREDIENTS:

- 2 kg beef brisket
- 50 ml olive oil
- 1 large red onion, chopped
- 4 cloves of garlic, minced
- 1 tbsp dried coriander
- 1 tbsp ground cumin
- 1 jalapeño pepper, sliced
- 75 g brown sugar
- 500 ml beef stock
- 200 ml red wine
- 200 g tinned chopped tomatoes
- 100 ml orange juice
- Salt and pepper

METHOD:

1. Heat the olive oil in a frying pan and when the oil is sizzling add in the onion, allowing them to soften and become translucent.

2. Add the garlic, cumin, coriander, jalapeños and sugar to the pan and cook for a further minute or two before removing from the heat and allowing the mixture to cool.

3. Season it with salt and pepper to taste.

4. Take your brisket and rub your cooled mixture all over, ensuring it is all covered. Place in a dish and allow it to refrigerate overnight.

5. The next morning, preheat your oven to 140 degrees Celsius.

6. Place the brisket into a roasting dish and in a separate bowl mix together your beef stock, red wine, tinned tomatoes and orange juice. Pour the liquid over the brisket and cover the roasting tin with a large piece of foil.

7. Cook the brisket in the oven for 2 and a half hours, then remove it from the oven. Turn the meat and return to the oven for another 2 and a half hours.

8. Remove it from the oven, ensuring the meat is cooked through and tender and then allow it to rest for twenty to thirty minutes. Set aside the cooking liquid to use later.

9. When you are ready to serve, place the brisket on the BBQ grill for five minutes on each side, allowing it to infuse with the chargrilled flavours. Regularly baste the meat with your retained cooking liquid while it is on the grill to ensure that it remains tender.

10. Remove from the grill and allow it to rest for a few minutes, then serve.

PER SERVING:

Calories: 600 | Carbs: 3 g | Fat: 28 g | Protein: 76 g

BBQ HOT DOGS

These American-style hot dogs are rich in taste and flavour. Ideal for popping into a hot dog bun and drizzling with mustard or ketchup, once you have sampled these delights you may never want to cook your hot dogs any other way.

Time: **20 minutes** | Serves: **4**

INGREDIENTS:

- ◆ 8 hot dogs (from a jar) or 8 sausages
- ◆ 8 hot dog buns

METHOD:

1. Heat your BBQ grill and place the hot dogs or sausages onto the cooking surface.

2. Cook for 5-6 minutes, watching as the hot dogs start to brown and chargrilled lines appear on the surface of the hot dogs.

3. Remove from the heat using tongs and place the hot dog in a bun and serve with mustard or ketchup.

PER SERVING:

Calories: 320 | Carbs: 4 g | Fat: 26 g | Protein: 12 g

SLOW-COOKED PORK BELLY

The succulent meat of this slow-cooked BBQ pork belly will melt in your mouth. Easy and simple to prepare, it will be a winner with everyone.

Time: **6 hours** | Serves: **4**

INGREDIENTS:

- 1.5 kg pork belly
- 1 medium white onion, chopped
- 300 ml cider
- 2 tsp English mustard
- 1 tsp paprika
- 2 cloves of garlic, minced
- 10 g brown sugar
- ½ tsp chilli powder
- Olive oil

METHOD:

1. In a bowl, mix together the mustard, paprika, minced garlic, brown sugar and chilli powder.

2. Coat the outside of the pork belly with the rub and transfer to a bowl or plastic bag, then place in the refrigerator to sit overnight.

3. The next day, preheat your own to 160 degrees Celsius.

4. In a large roasting tin, place your pork belly and onions and add in the cider.

5. Cover the tin with foil and allow it to roast in the oven for 4 hours until the meat is extremely tender.

6. Remove from the oven and baste the meat with olive oil.

7. Fire up your BBQ and allow it to come up to temperature.

8. Place the pork on the grill and, if you have a lid, cover the BBQ. However, if you do not have a BBQ with a lid, you can cook it on an open grill.

9. Allow it to cook on a low heat over the grill for 1 hour before serving. Ensure you turn the meat regularly and do not allow it to overcook.

PER SERVING:

Calories: 460 | Carbs: 1 g | Fat: 38 g | Protein: 61 g

HOMEMADE BEEF BURGERS

Homemade beef burgers are an ideal BBQ treat. The grill imbues them with an essence of the chargrilled flavour, enhancing the natural succulence of the meat and providing you with a taste sensation.

Time: **40 minutes** | Serves: **6**

INGREDIENTS:

- ◆ 500 g beef mince
- ◆ 6 burger buns
- ◆ 2 tbsp BBQ sauce (homemade or bought)
- ◆ 1 small white onion, chopped
- ◆ 2 cloves of garlic, minced
- ◆ 1 tsp salt
- ◆ 1 tsp black pepper
- ◆ ½ little gem lettuce
- ◆ 2 beefsteak tomatoes
- ◆ Cucumber slices
- ◆ 6 slices of Cheddar cheese (optional)
- ◆ 12 slices of pickles (optional)

METHOD:

1. In a large clean bowl, place your beef mince, onions, garlic, salt, pepper and the BBQ sauce.

2. Combine all the ingredients, ensuring that it is mixed thoroughly and that there is an even distribution throughout the mixture.

3. Using your hands, shape scoops of the mixture into 6 burger-shaped patties.

4. Heat your BBQ to a medium heat and place the burger patties onto the grill.

5. Cook for between 10 and 15 minutes on each side, depending on how well-done you want the burgers to be.

6. When the burgers are almost cooked, heat the buns on the grill, allowing them to toast slightly.

7. If you are adding cheese, place a slice of cheese on the burgers around a minute before they have finished cooking.

8. When the burgers are ready to eat, take a bun, place some lettuce on the bottom half and place the burger on the top of it. Add a slice of tomato and 2 slices of cucumber. If you are using pickles, top with a couple of slices of pickle.

9. Drizzle your sauce of choice, such as ketchup, mustard, mayonnaise or BBQ sauce over the top and close the bun with the top half.

10. Serve and enjoy.

PER SERVING:

Calories: 620 | Carbs: 28 g | Fat: 32 g | Protein: 38 g

SWEET AND STICKY CHILLI CHICKEN WINGS

A recipe that is inspired by American-style cooking, these chicken wings can be eaten off a plate or stuffed inside a soft tortilla wrap or pita bread. The sumptuous combination of sweet honey contrasts with the deep, rich and spicy flavours of the chilli to produce a dish that will leave your tastebuds tingling.

Time: **90 minutes** | Serves: **10**

INGREDIENTS:

- 20 fresh chicken wings
- 120 g flour
- 1 tsp chilli powder
- ½ tsp salt
- 1 tsp black pepper
- 2 tsp paprika
- 1 tsp garlic powder
- 20 chicken wings, or drumettes
- 250 g BBQ sauce
- 150 g honey

METHOD:

1. Preheat the oven to 220 degrees Celsius.

2. In a large bowl, mix together the flour, chilli powder, salt, black pepper, paprika and garlic powder, ensuring that all the ingredients are fully combined.

3. Dip each individual wing into the flour mixture, making sure that the wing is fully coated with the powder.

4. Place the coated wings on a greased baking tray and place them into the oven to cook for 45 minutes, turning them halfway through cooking.

5. While the wings are cooking, mix together the BBQ sauce and the honey.

6. When the wings have cooked, remove them from the oven and coat them in the sweet and sticky combined mixture of BBQ sauce and honey.

7. Heat your BBQ grill and place the wings onto the grill surface. Grill for 15 minutes, turning regularly and serve.

PER SERVING:

Calories: 420 | Carbs: 12 g | Fat: 18 g | Protein: 22 g

BEEF KEBAB SKEWERS

Can there be anything better than a skewer full of tender meat and grilled veggies? This recipe offers a delectable taste combination, perfect for BBQ connoisseurs.

Time: **40 minutes** | Serves: **4**

INGREDIENTS:

- 4 sirloin steaks, cut into cubes
- 50 ml olive oil
- 80 ml soy sauce
- 40 ml lemon juice
- 20 ml cider vinegar
- 30 ml Worcestershire sauce
- 20 ml honey
- 2 tsp Dijon mustard
- 200 g chestnut mushrooms, quartered
- 1 red pepper, chopped into cubes
- 1 green pepper, chopped into cubes
- 1 red onion, chopped into large cubes
- 8 cloves of garlic

METHOD:

1. The night before your BBQ, prepare the marinade for the beef by combining the olive oil, soy sauce, lemon juice, cider vinegar, Worcestershire sauce, honey and mustard in a large bowl.

2. Coat the cubes of beef steak in the marinade and allow the flavours to infuse by refrigerating the beef in the marinade overnight.

3. The next day, remove the beef from the fridge and allow it to come up to room temperature.

4. Heat your BBQ and while it is heating, take some kebab skewers and start to assemble the kebabs.

5. Place a cube of red pepper at the end of one skewer, followed by a cube of beef, then a slice of onion, then another cube of beef, then a cube of mushroom, then another cube of beef, then a garlic clove and another cube of beef.

6. Repeat until each skewer is filled with beef and veggies.

7. Lightly baste the skewers with some olive oil and season with black pepper before placing them on the BBQ grill.

8. Grill the kebabs for around 8-10 minutes, turning during cooking. Cooking time will vary, depending on how rare or well-done you prefer your beef steak to be.

9. Remove the skewers from the BBQ and rest for 5 minutes to allow them to fully finish cooking.

10. Serve with a side dish and a sauce.

PER SERVING:

Calories: 220 | Carbs: 4 g | Fat: 12 g | Protein: 12 g

SLOW-COOKED LAMB

Lamb is a meat that perfectly lends itself to BBQ cooking. Slow-cooked on the grill, it is a dish that is definitely worth waiting for! If you are hosting a late afternoon or evening BBQ, this slow-cooked lamb will be the perfect food to serve. You can leave it cooking on the grill all day long so that it will be ready to serve when your guests arrive.

Time: **10 hours** | Serves: **4**

INGREDIENTS:

- 1.5 kg lamb shoulder with the bone removed
- 2 medium white or brown onions, sliced
- 2 tsp black pepper
- 1 tsp ground coriander
- 1 ½ tsp curry powder
- 1 tsp ground mace
- 1 tsp salt
- 2 cloves of garlic, sliced
- 2 tsp dried rosemary
- 2 tsp dried thyme

METHOD:

1. Preheat your BBQ to a medium heat or 160 degrees Celsius.

2. In a large bowl, combine the black pepper, coriander, curry powder, mace, salt, rosemary and thyme.

3. Take a large piece of aluminium foil and place the lamb shoulder on the top of it.

4. Rub the spice mixture onto the outside of the lamb, ensuring that is it completely covered with the mix of herbs and spices. Place the slices of onion on the top of the lamb.

5. Fold up each side of the foil and seal well at the top.

6. Transfer the foil parcel with the lamb inside onto the BBQ grill and close the lid of the BBQ.

7. Cook the meat for 1 hour before reducing the heat to a low heat (around 80 degrees Celsius) and close the lid again. Leave to slow cook for around 7 hours.

8. When the lamb has been cooking for 8 hours in total, open up the foil and uses the juices in the foil to baste the meat. Turn the heat back up to medium or 160 degrees Celsius. Leaving the foil and the BBQ lid open, allow it to cook for one more hour before removing it from the grill.

9. Allow the lamb to rest for 20-30 minutes before serving.

PER SERVING:

Calories: 420 | Carbs: 2 g | Fat: 26 g | Protein: 18 g

SPICY BBQ SALMON

A fish-lovers delight, this spiced salmon is rich in flavours and spices. Offering a melt-in-the-mouth taste experience, one bite and you will be hooked.

Time: **30 minutes** | Serves: **4**

INGREDIENTS:

- 4 salmon fillets with the skin left on
- 1 tbsp hot chilli powder
- 2 tbsp cider vinegar
- 1 tbsp garlic paste
- 2 tsp ginger paste
- 2 tbsp lemon juice
- 1 tsp salt
- 1 tsp black pepper
- 1 tsp white sugar
- 20 ml olive oil

METHOD:

1. In a bowl, whisk together the chilli powder, cider vinegar, garlic paste, ginger paste, lemon juice, salt, black pepper, sugar and olive oil.

2. Heat your BBQ grill and place the salmon fillets on the grill with the skin side down.

3. Baste the salmon with the chilli mixture and cook for around 5 minutes before turning the salmon. Brush the fillets with more of the prepared glaze and cook for a further 2-3 minutes.

4. Remove the salmon from the heat and pour a little of the chilli glaze over the top to serve.

PER SERVING:

Calories: 290 | Carbs: 4 g | Fat: 12 g | Protein: 16 g

GRILLED SARDINES

These little fish provide huge flavour when grilled on the BBQ. Simple and easy to prepare, you will find that these are a tremendous hit with your guests.

Time: **40 minutes** | Serves: **5**

INGREDIENTS:

- 10 sardine fillets
- 60 ml lemon juice
- 60 ml olive oil
- 1 tsp smoked paprika
- ½ tsp black pepper
- 1 tsp sea salt
- 2 tbsp fresh parsley, chopped
- 4 cloves of garlic, minced
- Lemon wedges, for serving

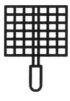

METHOD:

1. In a bowl, whisk together the garlic, olive oil, lemon juice, paprika, salt and black pepper.

2. Place the sardines into the bowl, making sure they are fully covered by the marinade and leave the flavours to infuse for 1 hour.

3. Preheat the BBQ and oil the grate before placing the sardine fillets onto the grill.

4. Grill for 2 minutes on each side, ensuring that the fish is cooked through before removing it and placing it onto plates.

5. Serve each fillet with a lemon wedge and your choice of side dish.

PER SERVING:

Calories: 220 | Carbs: 3 g | Fat: 6 g | Protein: 9 g

SPICY TEX-MEX FAJITAS

Made with tender strips of chicken and a delicious selection of vegetables, these are ideally suited to lovers of spices.

Time: **20 minutes** | Serves: **4**

INGREDIENTS:

- 4 chicken breast fillets, cut into thick strips
- 4 flour tortilla wraps
- 1 large white onion, chopped
- 80 ml olive oil
- 2 tbsp lime juice
- 2 tbsp chilli powder
- 2 tbsp ground cumin
- 2 tsp salt
- 1 tbsp black pepper
- 2 tsp paprika
- 2 tsp dried oregano
- 1 tsp onion powder
- 2 tsp garlic powder
- 1 tsp dried parsley
- ½ head of lettuce
- Sour Cream
- Guacamole
- Tomato salsa
- Grated cheddar cheese

METHOD:

1. In a large clean bowl, combine the chilli powder, ground cumin, salt, pepper, paprika, dried oregano, onion powder and dried parsley.

2. In a separate bowl, whisk together the olive oil and the lime juice and then add in your dry chilli mixture. Whisk thoroughly until everything is fully mixed and there are no lumps.

3. Place the strips of chicken breast into a bowl or a zip lock bag, and pour the marinade over the meat. Refrigerate for at least 6 hours or overnight.

4. Remove the chicken from the fridge and preheat the BBQ grill to a medium heat. Cook the chicken on the grill for at least 5 minutes before turning the strips and cooking for another 5 minutes.

5. While the chicken is cooking, toast the tortilla wraps on the BBQ for 1-2 minutes to warm them and give them a chargrilled appearance.

6. When the chicken juices run clear, remove them from the grill.

7. Assemble the fajitas by layering lettuce, strips of chicken and your favourite sauces inside the wraps and top with grated cheese before serving.

PER SERVING:

Calories: 485 | Carbs: 28 g | Fat: 19 g | Protein: 20 g

VEGETARIAN AND VEGAN OPTIONS

Vegetarians and vegans can enjoy the delicious flavours of BBQ cooking too. This exciting range of vegetarian and vegan mains will also have meat-eaters eager for a taste too. Adults and kids alike will find it difficult to resist these delectable veggie and vegan meals.

FALAFEL BURGERS

Inspired by Middle Eastern cooking, this fusion dish brings together exotic flavours to keep everyone happy. Fully vegan, they are an excellent option to include on your menu to ensure that there is a dish to serve everyone when you host a cookout.

Time: **25 minutes** | Serves: **4**

INGREDIENTS:

- 400 g can of chickpeas, drained and rinsed under cold water
- 1 large red onion, diced
- 2 cloves of garlic, minced
- 1 tsp dried coriander
- 2 tsp dried parsley
- 1 tsp cumin
- 1 tsp chilli powder
- 10 g plain flour
- ½ tsp salt
- 1 tsp black pepper
- 50 ml olive oil
- 4 burger buns
- 2 beefsteak tomatoes
- ½ head of little gem lettuce

METHOD:

1. Rinse and fully dry the chickpeas before placing them into a blender. Add in the onion, garlic, parsley, cumin, coriander, chilli powder and plain flour.

2. Blend the mixture until it is smooth but still retains some texture. Carefully transfer it from the blender to a bowl.

3. Using your hands, scoop a handful of the mixture, roll it into a ball and then flatten to make the shape of a burger patty. Make four separate patties from the mixture.

4. Preheat the BBQ to around 180 degrees Celsius or medium-high heat and brush the grill with oil. Place the burger patties onto the grill and cook for 8-10 minutes on either side until the patties have firmed up and are cooked through.

5. While the burgers are cooking, toast the buns on the grill for 1-2 minutes to chargrill them and warm them.

6. Remove the burgers from the heat and layer the falafel burger, lettuce, a thick and juicy slice of tomato followed by a drizzle of your favourite burger sauce over the top.

7. Close the bun and serve.

PER SERVING:

Calories: 350 | Carbs: 26 g | Fat: 12 g | Protein: 14 g

GRILLED HALLOUMI

One of the most versatile cheeses, halloumi is perfect for popping onto your grill. It retains its shape and absorbs the chargrilled flavours to deliver a winning taste experience.

Time: **20 minutes** | Serves: **4**

INGREDIENTS:

- 500 g halloumi cheese
- 2 tbsp olive oil
- 1 tbsp mixed Italian herb seasoning
- ½ tsp black pepper

METHOD:

1. Soak the halloumi cheese in cold water for 4 hours to remove some of the salt content as this will deliver a better flavour.
2. Remove the cheese from the water and pat it dry. Then, slice into thick slices about 1.5 inches in thickness.
3. Coat the halloumi with olive oil and season with the mixed Italian herbs and black pepper.
4. Preheat the BBQ grill to a medium heat and place the slices of halloumi onto the grill.
5. Cook for 3 minutes before turning the cheese and cooking for a further 3 minutes on the other side.
6. Remove from the grill and serve.

PER SERVING:

Calories: 550 | Carbs: 2 g | Fat: 42g | Protein: 7 g

BBQ AUBERGINE

Delicious as a main course or served as a side in smaller portions, this BBQ aubergine recipe is tantalising and will prove extremely popular among your family members and friends.

Time: **40 minutes** | Serves: **4**

INGREDIENTS:

- 2 aubergines
- 2 tsp salt
- 60 ml olive oil
- 3 cloves of garlic, minced
- 2 tbsp fresh parsley, chopped
- 2 tbsp fresh oregano
- ½ tsp black pepper
- ½ tsp salt

METHOD:

1. Slice the aubergine into thick slices around 1 cm in thickness and season each slice with a sprinkle of salt allowing the salt to draw any moisture from the aubergine.

2. Rest the aubergine slices for 20 minutes and then pat them dry with a clean cloth.

3. Preheat the BBQ to a medium heat or 180 degrees Celsius.

4. While the BBQ is heating, in a bowl combine the olive oil, minced garlic, parsley, oregano, black pepper and ½ tsp of salt. Mix it thoroughly.

5. Dip the aubergine slices into the mixture, ensuring that every slice is fully coated.

6. Place the slices of aubergine onto the grill and allow them to cook for 5-6 minutes on each side.

7. Remove from the grill and drizzle some of the oil and garlic mixture over the top to make them moist and tender before serving.

PER SERVING:

Calories: 380 | Carbs: 8 g | Fat: 19 g | Protein: 8 g

VEGGIE KEBABS

Lucious mushrooms, tomatoes and courgettes form the basis for this summery vegetarian treat. Chargrilled to perfection, it is a delicious meal that can be eaten for lunch or dinner.

Time: **30 minutes** | Serves: **4**

INGREDIENTS:

- 400 g button mushrooms, cleaned
- 2 large red onions, chopped
- 1 green bell pepper, diced
- 1 red bell pepper, diced
- 1 courgette, cubed
- 8 cloves of garlic, sliced into halves
- 200 g cherry tomatoes
- 80 ml olive oil
- 1 tsp dried oregano
- 1 tsp dried parsley
- 1 tsp dried basil
- ½ tsp salt
- 1 tsp black pepper
- 1 tbsp lemon juice

METHOD:

1. Combine the olive oil, oregano, parsley, basil, salt and pepper and lemon juice in a large bowl.

2. Preheat your BBQ to a medium heat of around 180 degrees Celsius.

3. Take some kebab skewers and layer the vegetables and garlic pieces alternately onto the skewers until you have filled 8-12 separate skewers.

4. Drizzle the olive oil mixture over the prepared skewers or use a brush to apply it.

5. Place the skewers onto the grill for 15 minutes, turning halfway during cooking.

6. Remove the skewers from the grill, drizzle with a little more of the olive oil mixture and serve.

PER SERVING:

Calories: 210 | Carbs: 22 g | Fat: 10 g | Protein: 4 g

EASY CHEESY BEAN BURGERS

Easy to prepare and fantastic to eat, these veggie bean burgers are flavoured with subtle herbs and spices.

Time: **25 minutes** | Serves: **4**

INGREDIENTS:

- 180 g cooked quinoa
- 400 g black beans, rinsed
- 150 g almonds
- 20 ml olive oil
- 150 g sweet potato, peeled and sliced
- 300 g button mushrooms
- ½ tsp salt
- 2 tsp chilli powder
- 2 tsp cumin powder
- 50 g cheddar cheese
- 4 burger buns
- Lettuce leaves
- 1 beefsteak tomato, sliced

METHOD:

1. Preheat your oven to 180 degrees Celsius and place the black beans onto a lined baking tray.

2. Bake the beans for 5 minutes, then remove from the oven and place the almonds onto the baking tray with the beans. Bake for another 8-10 minutes until the nuts are golden brown but not burnt.

3. Remove the tray from the oven and allow the beans and nuts to cool.

4. Meanwhile, add some oil to a large frying pan and heat over a medium heat on the stove. Add in the sweet potatoes and cook for 4 minutes before turning and cooking for a further 4 minutes. Remove the pan from the heat and set the sweet potatoes aside to cool.

5. Return the pan to the heat and add in the mushrooms, frying for 5 minutes until they have browned, then remove the pan from the heat and allow the mushrooms to cool.

6. In a blender, place the cooled beans and almonds and blitz them until they are ground but not loose. The mix should still retain some texture.

7. Into the blender, add the sweet potatoes, the mushrooms, half the quinoa, the salt, pepper, chilli powder and cumin. Blend the mixture to combine but do not overdo it or it will become too loose.

8. Transfer the mixture to a clean bowl and stir in the rest of the quinoa. If the mixture is not firm enough to can add in more

quinoa until you achieve the right texture.

9. Divide the mixture into four and scoop up one-quarter of the mixture into your hands. Take a cube of cheddar cheese and roll the mixture into a ball with the cheese cube at its centre, then flatten into a patty shape. Repeat this until you have four patties.

10. Place the burger patties onto a plate and loosely cover with cling wrap before putting them into the fridge to chill for one hour.

11. When you are ready to cook the patties, preheat the BBQ and brush the grill with oil.

12. Cook the patties for 10-12 minutes on each side.

13. When the burgers are almost ready, toast the buns for 1-2 minutes on the grill, then remove the buns and patties to assemble.

14. Place the bean burgers onto the buns and add some lettuce leaves and a slice of tomato on the top. Close the buns and serve.

PER SERVING:

Calories: 310 | Carbs: 45 g | Fat: 21 g | Protein: 11 g

MINI BBQ PIZZAS

If you have never tried pizzas grilled on a BBQ, now is the time to start. A unique twist on the traditional Italian dish, they are great as a vegetarian option or they can be served as a starter or canapes.

Time: **140 minutes** | Serves: **4**

INGREDIENTS:

- 7 g dried active baking yeast
- ½ tsp white sugar
- 1 ½ tsp salt
- 15 ml olive oil
- 400 g plain flour
- 240 ml warm water
- 2 cloves of garlic, minced
- 2 tbsp tomato puree
- 2 tbsp passata
- 200 g mozzarella cheese, grated
- 3 tbsp fresh basil, chopped
- Your own choice of veggies for toppings (optional)

METHOD:

1. Pour the warm water into a large clean bowl and allow the yeast to dissolve in it.

2. Mix in the sugar and leave the solution to sit for 10-15 minutes until it begins to become frothy.

3. Mix in the salt, half the olive oil and plain flour and work the mixture into a dough.

4. Flour a clean surface and transfer the dough from the bowl to the floured surface.

5. Knead the dough vigorously until it is smooth for around 10 minutes, then transfer to an oiled bowl, cover with a damp cloth and leave it to double in size.

6. When the dough has doubled in size, knead it again, working the minced garlic paste through the dough. Return it to the bowl, recover and set it aside to allow it to rise again.

7. Preheat your BBQ to a high heat or 220 degrees Celsius and brush the grill with oil.

8. Divide your pizza dough into 8 balls and flatten each ball into the shape of a mini pizza base.

9. Place the bases onto the BBQ allowing them to fluff up, which should only take 1-2 minutes, then flip the bases and brush with a little oil before topping them with the tomato puree, passata, basil, cheese and any other choice of toppings that you have selected.

10. Close the BBQ lid and allow the pizzas to cook until the mozzarella is melted and gooey, then remove from the grill and serve.

PER SERVING:

Calories: 220 | Carbs: 28 g | Fat: 16 g | Protein: 6 g

YEE-HAW SIDES

A BBQ feast is not complete without a range of delightful side dishes. Designed to perfectly complement the meat, fish and veggie main dishes, you can even serve these sides as a starter or as canapes while everyone is waiting for their main courses to come off the grill.

GARLICKY CORN ON THE COB

A traditional BBQ side with a modern twist. Garlicky corn on the cob is perfect on the side of any BBQ main.

Time: **40 minutes** | Serves: **6**

INGREDIENTS:

- 6 whole corn cobs
- 1 tbsp honey
- 1 tbsp tomato ketchup
- 120 g unsalted butter
- 1 tsp chilli powder
- 3 cloves of garlic, minced
- Salt and pepper to season

METHOD:

1. In a large bowl, mix together the butter, tomato ketchup, honey, garlic, chilli powder, and salt and pepper until the mixture is smooth and without any lumps.

2. Lay two sheets of foil down on top of each other for each corn cob and wrap them around the cobs.

3. Place the foil-wrapped corn cobs onto a preheated BBQ grill for 35 minutes, leaving on longer if you prefer a more chargrilled flavour.

4. Carefully unwrap the foil and serve the corn cobs with extra butter on the side.

PER SERVING:

Calories: 180 | Carbs: 12 g | Fat: 6 g | Protein: 2 g

BBQ SWEET POTATOES

Healthy and satisfying, these sweet potatoes are crispy on the outside and soft and fluffy on the inside. With deep and rich chargrilled flavours, they provide an ideal accompaniment to burgers and fish dishes.

Time: **45 minutes** | Serves: **4**

INGREDIENTS:

- 4 large sweet potatoes, peeled and whole
- 1 tbsp olive oil
- 2 tbsp chopped chives
- Salt and pepper

METHOD:

1. Coat each sweet potato with olive oil, season with salt and pepper and sprinkle over some chives.

2. Wrap each potato in a double layer of aluminium foil.

3. Place the foil-wrapped potatoes onto the preheated grill on a medium heat for 15-20 minutes then turn and cook for a further 20 minutes.

4. Unwrap the potatoes and serve with butter or a dip.

PER SERVING:

Calories: 140 | Carbs: 26 g | Fat: 2 g | Protein: 1 g

LEMONY COURGETTES

Low in calories and high in taste, this quick and easy dish is great for whipping up on the grill in minutes.

Time: **25 minutes** | Servings: **4**

INGREDIENTS:

- 2 medium courgettes, sliced lengthways (1 cm thick)
- 1 tbsp olive oil
- 1 tbsp cider lemon juice
- 1 tbsp mixed Italian herbs seasoning
- 1 tsp garlic powder
- ½ tsp salt
- ½ tsp black pepper

METHOD:

1. Combine olive oil, lemon juice, herbs, garlic powder, salt and pepper together in a bowl.

2. Cover the courgette slices with the oil mixture, making sure each slice is fully coated.

3. Brush a preheated medium-heat BBQ grill with oil and place the slices of courgette directly onto the grill.

4. Close the lid and cook for 2 minutes before turning and cooking for a further 2 minutes.

5. Remove the courgettes from the grill with tongs and serve.

PER SERVING:

Calories: 130 | Carbs: 8 g | Fat: 4 g | Protein: 1 g

AMERICAN-STYLE SLAW

Simple to pre-prepare ready for your BBQ, American style slaw takes coleslaw to a whole new level. This dish takes its inspiration from the Southern states and will liven up your BBQ.

Time: **20 minutes** | Servings: **4**

INGREDIENTS:

- 120 g full-fat mayonnaise
- 1 tbsp French mustard
- 2 tbsp caster sugar
- 2 tbsp white wine vinegar
- 1 tsp onion powder
- ½ tsp garlic powder
- ½ tsp salt
- ½ tsp white pepper
- 1/4 white cabbage, thinly chopped
- 1/4 red cabbage, thinly chopped
- 1 large carrot, grated lengthways
- 1/4 red onion, thinly sliced

METHOD:

1. Blanch the onion slices in a bowl of boiling water for 10 minutes, before draining and drying with a clean cloth.

2. Mix together the mayonnaise, mustard, caster sugar, vinegar, onion powder, garlic powder, salt and pepper in a bowl, making sure all the ingredients are fully combined.

3. Stir in the grated carrot, onion and cabbage and allow the mayonnaise mixture to fully coat the vegetables before serving.

PER SERVING:

Calories: 130 | Carbs: 4 g | Fat: 8 g | Protein: 1 g

BBQ BABY POTATOES

Time: **20 minutes** | Serves: **8**

For an impressive side that takes little work, these tasty moreish treats will do the trick.

INGREDIENTS:

- ◆ 1 kg baby potatoes
- ◆ 3 tbsp olive oil
- ◆ Salt and pepper
- ◆ Butter, to serve

METHOD:

1. Par-boil the baby potatoes in a saucepan full of boiling water for 10 minutes, then drain and allow the potatoes to steam dry.

2. Toss the dry potatoes in olive oil, fully coating them.

3. Lay out a large sheet of aluminium foil and spread the potatoes across the sheet. Season the potatoes with salt and pepper.

4. Wrap the foil, covering all the potatoes, then transfer to a medium-hot BBQ grill for 10-15 minutes before serving with butter on the side.

PER SERVING:

Calories: 140 | Carbs: 21 g | Fat: 4 g | Protein: 3 g

TEXAS RICE SALAD

Whip up this salad the day before your BBQ and store it in the refrigerator to allow the flavours time to mature.

Time: **50 minutes** | Serves: **4**

INGREDIENTS:

- 400 g cooked brown rice
- 40 ml lemon juice
- 60 ml olive oil
- 1 tbsp honey
- ¼ tsp chilli powder
- ¼ tsp garlic powder
- ¼ tsp cumin powder
- ½ tsp salt
- ½ tsp black pepper
- 1 red bell pepper, de-seeded and diced
- 1 green bell pepper, de-seeded and diced
- 1 red onion, diced
- 1 tomato, finely diced
- A handful of fresh parsley, finely chopped
- A handful of fresh coriander, finely chopped

METHOD:

1. In a large bowl, mix together the lemon juice, olive oil, honey, chilli powder, garlic powder, cumin powder, salt and black pepper, thoroughly combining all the ingredients.

2. Toss in the green and red bell peppers, onion, tomato, parsley and coriander and serve.

PER SERVING:

Calories: 110 | Carbs: 22 g | Fat: 6 g | Protein: 4 g

CHARGRILLED CAULIFLOWER

With its firm texture and delicious flavours, cauliflower is ideal for grilling.

Time: **30 minutes** | Serves: **2-4**

INGREDIENTS:

- 1 head of cauliflower
- 1 tbsp olive oil
- 2 tbsp lemon juice
- 2 cloves of garlic, minced
- 1 tsp honey
- 1 tsp sea salt
- ¼ tsp chilli flakes
- A handful of fresh parsley, chopped

METHOD:

1. Prepare the cauliflower by cutting it into thick (2 cm) slices lengthways.

2. In a clean bowl, mix together the oil, lemon juice, minced garlic, honey, sea salt, chilli flakes and parsley.

3. Coat the cauliflower slices with the oil mixture and leave the flavours to infuse for 1 hour.

4. On a medium-hot grill that has been brushed with oil, place the cauliflower slices and leave them to cook for 5 minutes.

5. Using tongs, flip the cauliflower and cook on the other side.

6. Remove from the grill and serve piping hot.

PER SERVING:

Calories: 180 | Carbs: 16 g | Fat: 7 g | Protein: 9 g

GRILLED MUSHROOMS AND ASPARAGUS

This hot grilled salad combines the woody flavours of mushrooms with the rich and tangy taste of asparagus.

Time: **20 minutes** | Serves: **4**

INGREDIENTS:

- 400 g mushrooms, sliced
- 200 g fresh asparagus spears
- 60 ml olive oil
- 20 ml lemon juice
- 1 tsp garlic paste
- Salt and pepper to season

METHOD:

1. In a large bowl, mix together the olive oil, lemon juice and garlic paste and season with salt and pepper to taste.

2. Toss the mushrooms and the asparagus in the olive oil mixture.

3. Lay out a large sheet of foil and place the mushrooms and asparagus onto the foil, ensuring that the veggies are evenly spread.

4. Wrap the foil up into a parcel and place it onto a medium-hot BBQ grill.

5. Close the BBQ lid and cook for 20-25 minutes, then open the lid and remove the foil parcel from the grill.

6. Carefully unwrap the foil and serve the mushrooms and asparagus in a large dish.

PER SERVING:

Calories: 90 | Carbs: 8 g | Fat: 9 g | Protein: 4 g

DELICIOUS DIPS

BBQ just wouldn't be BBQ without some wonderful dips served on the side. This comprehensive range of dips will harmonise perfectly with just about any main or side dish that you serve.

BBQ SAUCE

The quintessential sauce to accompany any BBQ dish, this is a traditional recipe for BBQ sauce that everyone loves.

Time: **20 minutes** | Serves: **6**

INGREDIENTS:

- 600 ml tomato ketchup
- 800 ml apple cider vinegar
- 1 tsp salt
- 3 tbsp paprika
- 1 tbsp black treacle
- 3 tsp chilli powder
- 150 ml Worcestershire sauce
- 1 tsp cayenne pepper
- 4 cloves of garlic, minced

METHOD:

1. Add all the ingredients into a large saucepan and cook over a medium heat for 20 minutes until the sauce starts to thicken.
2. Sieve the sauce to remove any bits and allow it to cool.
3. Place in a clean bowl and refrigerate it overnight to allow the flavours to fully develop.

PER SERVING:

Calories: 90 | Carbs: 1 g | Fat: 3 g | Protein: 1 g

ONION RELISH

Perfect for serving on a burger or hot dog, you won't be able to resist the tangy and sweet combination of flavours offered by onion relish.

Time: **20 minutes** | Serves: **6**

INGREDIENTS:

- 2 red onions, thinly sliced
- 1 tbsp butter
- 1 tbsp olive oil
- ½ tsp salt
- ½ tsp black pepper
- 1 tsp honey
- 1 tbsp caster sugar
- 1 tbsp white wine vinegar

METHOD:

1. In a large frying pan, heat the butter and olive oil on the stove. When the butter and oil mixture is sizzling hot, add in the onions and cook for 5 minutes to soften.

2. Turn up the heat and add in the salt, pepper, sugar and honey.

3. Cook for a further 2 minutes, then pour in the white wine vinegar.

4. Leave the relish to cook on the stove, allowing it to reduce and thicken. When it is at your desired texture, remove the pan from the heat and transfer it to another container to cool.

PER SERVING:

Calories: 90 | Carbs: 11 g | Fat: 12 g | Protein: 1 g

SPICY TOMATO SALSA

Great for serving with Mexican and Tex-Mex dishes, spicy tomato salsa is not for the fainthearted. Bold and hot, you can adjust the spiciness to suit your personal tastes.

Time: **10 minutes** | Serves: **8**

INGREDIENTS:

- 400 g tin of chopped tomatoes
- 1 clove of garlic, chopped
- ½ medium white onion, diced
- 1 tsp dried coriander
- 1 small jalapeño pepper, de-seeded and thinly sliced
- 1 tbsp lime juice
- ½ tsp sea salt

METHOD:

1. Remove the tomatoes from the tin and drain around half of the excess juice.

2. Add the tomatoes, garlic, onion, coriander, jalapeños, lime juice and sea salt to a blender and pulse until the mixture is smooth but not pureed.

3. Transfer to a bowl and serve.

PER SERVING:

Calories: 65 | Carbs: 2 g | Fat: 4 g | Protein: 1 g

GUACAMOLE

This popular avocado-based dip is given a modern makeover in this dip recipe. Just when you thought guacamole could not get any better, it does!

Time: **10 minutes** | Serves: **6-8**

INGREDIENTS:

- 3 large, ripe avocados
- 1 ripe tomato
- 2 tbsp lime juice
- 1 red onion, diced
- A handful of coriander leaves, finely chopped
- 1 red chilli, de-seeded and chopped
- Salt and black pepper to season

METHOD:

1. Halve the avocados and remove the stone. Scoop out the flesh from each half and place in a blender with the tomato, onion, red chilli and coriander, pulsing very lightly until the mixture is texture but not runny.

2. Transfer the mixture from the blender to a bowl and stir in the lime juice. Season with salt and black pepper to taste before serving.

PER SERVING:

Calories: 110 | Carbs: 2 g | Fat: 10 g | Protein: 1 g

LIME MAYO

An easy mayonnaise with a citrusy twist.

Time: **20 minutes** | Serves: **6**

INGREDIENTS:

- 2 egg yolks
- 4 tbsp lime juice
- Zest of 2 limes
- 2 tsp English mustard
- 500 ml olive oil
- ½ tsp salt

METHOD:

1. In a large bowl, whisk together the egg yolks, lime juice, lime zest and English mustard using an electric mixer for 1-2 minutes.

2. Pour in the olive oil while continuing to whisk the mixture. Keep whisking for several minutes until the mixture thickens to the consistency of mayonnaise.

3. Season with ¼ tsp of salt, adding more or less according to your personal tastes, and serve.

PER SERVING:

Calories: 130 | Carbs: 4 g | Fat: 15 g | Protein: 4 g

NOTE: This recipe contains raw eggs and consequently it may not be suitable for infants, pregnant women and older adults.

CREAMY CUCUMBER RAITA

This dip harmonises perfectly with fish and vegetable dishes. Taking only minutes to prepare, it will be a huge hit at your BBQ.

Time: **10 minutes** | Serves: **6-8**

INGREDIENTS:

◆ 600 g thick Greek yoghurt
◆ 1 cucumber, peeled and diced with seeds removed
◆ 25 g fresh mint, chopped
◆ 35 g fresh coriander, chopped
◆ ½ tsp salt
◆ ¼ tsp white pepper

METHOD:

1. Put the yoghurt, mint, coriander, salt and white pepper into a blender and pulse until smooth.

2. Transfer the mixture to a bowl and stir the cucumber through it before serving.

PER SERVING:

Calories: 135 | Carbs: 8 g | Fat: 6 g | Protein: 6 g

GARLIC AND HERB MAYO

Perfect for potatoes, fish, meats and veggies, this delightful dip is a simple solution to a creamy craving for a BBQ dip.

Time: **10 minutes** | Serves: **4**

INGREDIENTS:

- 120 g full-fat mayonnaise
- 120 g sour cream
- 2 cloves of garlic, minced
- 1 tsp dried parsley
- 1 tsp dried coriander
- White pepper, to season

METHOD:

1. Stir the mayonnaise and sour cream together in a large bowl.

2. Add in the minced garlic, parsley and coriander and stir it through thoroughly.

3. Season to taste with white pepper.

PER SERVING:

Calories: 140 | Carbs: 8 g | Fat: 12 g | Protein: 2 g

HONEY MUSTARD DIP

Sweet and sharp, this dip will tantalise your tastebuds.

Time: **10 minutes** | Serves: **6**

INGREDIENTS:

- 90 g runny honey
- 90 g mayonnaise
- 60 g Dijon mustard
- 1 tbsp lemon juice
- ½ tsp cayenne pepper powder

METHOD:

In a large bowl mix together all the ingredients until thoroughly combined and then serve.

PER SERVING:

Calories: 85 | Carbs: 9 g | Fat: 4 g | Protein: 1 g

CHIPOTLE SAUCE

A smoky, mildly spicy dip, this is a perfect accompaniment to BBQ foods.

Time: **20 minutes** | Serves: **8**

INGREDIENTS:

- 30 g chipotle paste
- 120 ml sour cream
- 60 g mayonnaise
- 3 tbsp coriander, chopped
- 1 tsp garlic powder
- 1 tsp cayenne pepper powder
- ½ tsp cumin
- ¼ tsp salt

METHOD:

1. Blend all the ingredients in an electric blender.
2. Transfer to a bowl and serve.

PER SERVING:

Calories: 70 | Carbs: 6 g | Fat: 8 g | Protein: 1 g

DEVILISH DESSERTS

When you're looking for something sweet and satisfying, looking no further than these lovely BBQ desserts. They will impress guests and have everyone wanting a second helping. Perfect for summer, these sweet treats are BBQ delights.

BOOZY GRILLED BANANAS

Bananas are an excellent dessert to prepare on the BBQ grill. This rum-soaked treat will satisfy your cravings for something sweet at the end of your BBQ.

Time: **30 minutes** | Serves: **6**

INGREDIENTS:

- 6 bananas, unpeeled
- 60 g unsalted butter, softened
- 50 g dark muscovado sugar
- 1 tsp treacle
- 2 tbsp dark spiced rum

METHOD:

1. In a bowl, combine the butter, sugar, treacle and rum.

2. With the curved sides of the bananas point upwards, split each banana skin lengthways but do not slice the banana in half.

3. Pipe the sugary rum butter into the inside of the banana skins, ensuring that it is spread down the entire length of the fruits.

4. Wrap the bananas in aluminium foil, ensuring that you keep them with the curved side up to prevent the butter from leaking.

5. Place the foil parcel directly onto the charcoals of your BBQ and allow them to roast for 15 minutes, turning halfway during cooking.

6. Carefully remove the bananas from the BBQ and unwrap the foil before peeling the bananas and serving with ice cream or cream.

PER SERVING:

Calories: 260 | Carbs: 16 g | Fat: 17 g | Protein: 8 g

BBQ PINEAPPLES AND PEACHES

Grilled pineapple rings and juicy peach halves make for a stunning dessert hot off the grill.

Time: **20 minutes** | Serves: **4**

INGREDIENTS:

- 1 pineapple with the rind removed, sliced into 2 cm thick rings
- 2 fresh peaches, halved
- 100 g dark brown sugar

METHOD:

1. Coat the pineapple rings and peach halves with brown sugar.

2. Heat your BBQ to a medium heat and brush the grill with oil.

3. Place the pineapple rings and peach halves onto the grill and allow them to cook for 3-4 minutes on each side before removing them from the grill.

4. Serve piping hot with a scoop of ice cream.

PER SERVING:

Calories: 320 | Carbs: 8 g | Fat: 3 g | Protein: 1 g

CAMPFIRE GRILLED APPLES

Reminiscent of camping in the woods, these apples are smoky and deep in flavour. The rich caramel sauce provides a sweet and opulent contrast when drizzled over the soft yet crispy apples.

Time: **30 minutes** | Serves: **4**

INGREDIENTS:

- 4 gala apples
- 1 tbsp butter
- 2 tbsp brown sugar
- 1 tsp cinnamon powder
- 2 tbsp sultanas or raisins
- 2 tbsp almonds or pecans
- 1 tbsp rum

METHOD:

1. Core the apples, leaving the bottoms of the apples intact as this will stop the butter and filling from leaking when you fill the apples.

2. In a bowl, combine the butter, sugar, cinnamon, and rum, then mix in the sultanas or raisins and the nuts. Ensure that it is thoroughly mixed together.

3. Place a dollop of filling inside each of the apples, filling them to the very top.

4. Place each apple onto a square of foil and sprinkle a little more sugar onto the top. Transfer to the grill of a preheated BBQ and close the BBQ lid.

5. Allow the apples to cook for 20 minutes before opening the lid and remove them from the grill.

6. Serve the apples hot either on their own or with a scoop of ice cream.

PER SERVING:

Calories: 280 | Carbs: 19 g | Fat: 20 g | Protein: 2 g

FRUIT KEBABS

A grilled fruit salad on a stick!

Time: **25 minutes** | Serves: **4**

INGREDIENTS:

- 1 pineapple, skin removed and flesh cubed
- 2 peaches, peeled and cubed
- 200 g strawberries
- 1 apple, peeled, cored and cubed
- 100 g grapes
- 1 tbsp honey

METHOD:

1. Take 8-12 skewers and layer the fruit cubes alternately along the skewers until each one is full and brush the fruit with honey.

2. Place the skewers onto a preheated BBQ grill over a medium heat.

3. Allow the skewers to cook for 8-10 minutes before flipping and cooking for a further 8-10 minutes, then serve.

PER SERVING:

Calories: 180 | Carbs: 22 g | Fat: 3 g | Protein: 2 g

AMERICAN STYLE S'MORES

What more could you ask for in a BBQ dessert than crunch biscuits, luxurious chocolate and rich melted marshmallows.

Time: **10 minutes** | Serves: **4**

INGREDIENTS:

- 8 rich tea biscuits
- 4 pieces of milk chocolate
- 4 marshmallows

METHOD:

1. Take 2 rich tea biscuits and sandwich a piece of milk chocolate and a marshmallow between them.
2. Wrap the biscuit sandwich in foil and repeat with the other three.
3. Place the foil parcels onto a hot BBQ grill for 4 minutes, turning halfway.
4. Remove from the grill, unwrap and enjoy!

PER SERVING:

Calories: 170 | Carbs: 16 g | Fat: 7 g | Protein: 1 g

AMERICAN-STYLE CHOCOLATE BROWNIES

The perfect end to your BBQ, these chocolate brownies can be pre-prepared the day before to ensure that you deliver the sweetest of treats to your guests.

Time: **60 minutes** | Serves: **8**

INGREDIENTS:

- 180 g butter
- 180 g dark chocolate
- 3 eggs
- 240 g caster sugar
- 70 g plain flour
- 25 g cocoa powder
- 45 g pecans
- 1 tsp vanilla extract

METHOD:

1. Preheat the oven to 180 degrees Celsius and grease a large, square baking tin.

2. Melt the chocolate in the microwave or in a bowl above a pan of boiling water, then allow it to cool a little.

3. Meanwhile, whisk together the eggs and the sugar using an electric mixer, until the mixture is creamy and smooth.

4. Pour in the cooled chocolate mixture and fold it through the whipped eggs and sugar.

5. Using a sieve, sift the flour and cocoa into the rest of the batter and carefully fold it in.

6. Stir in the vanilla and the nuts and transfer to your baking tin.

7. Bake in the oven for 25 minutes, then remove and allow the brownies to cool in the tin completely before cutting and serving.

PER SERVING:

Calories: 380 | Carbs: 26 g | Fat: 17 g | Protein: 4 g

MELON SKEWERS

Made with cubes of cantaloupe melon, the sweet melon soaks up the chargrilled flavours to deliver a taste sensation.

Time: **10 minutes** | Serves: **4**

INGREDIENTS:

- 1 cantaloupe melon, cut into cubes
- 1 tbsp honey

METHOD:

1. Stack your melon cubes onto a skewer and thoroughly brush with honey.

2. Place the skewers onto a hot BBQ grill and cook for 2-3 minutes before turning and cooking for another 2-3 minutes before serving.

PER SERVING:

Calories: 85 | Carbs: 9 g | Fat: 1 g | Protein: 1 g

STRAWBERRY CRUMBLE

Swift to prepare and simple to assemble, this dessert is an ideal summer treat that is delicious on its own or when served with whipped cream or ice cream.

Time: **60 minutes** | Serves: **6**

INGREDIENTS:

- 400 g strawberries, sliced
- 200 g plain flour
- ½ tsp salt
- 180 g butter
- 130 g brown sugar
- 45 g rolled oats
- 40 g ground almonds
- 1 tbsp caster sugar
- 1 tsp vanilla extract
- 180 ml double cream
- 80 g plain Greek yoghurt
- 2 tbsp icing sugar

METHOD:

1. Preheat the oven to 180 degrees Celsius.

2. In a large bowl, mix together the flour, salt, butter, brown sugar, oats and ground almonds until they become combined and crumbly.

3. On a greased and lined baking tray, lay out the crumble mixture and bake for 20-25 minutes.

4. Meanwhile, whip together the double cream, caster sugar, vanilla and Greek yoghurt with an electric mixer until the mixture thickens.

5. Lay out a sheet of foil and place your sliced strawberries on it before wrapping it into a parcel.

6. Place the strawberry parcels onto a preheated, medium-hot BBQ grill and allow them to cool for 10 minutes before removing.

7. Remove your crumble topping from the oven and set it aside.

8. Transfer your grilled strawberries from the foil to a large serving bowl and then spoon on the cream and yoghurt mixture, spreading it evenly across the top of the strawberries.

9. Top with shards of the baked crumble mixture and serve.

PER SERVING:

Calories: 240 | Carbs: 22 g | Fat: 18 g | Protein: 9 g

Disclaimer

This book contains opinions and ideas of the author and is meant to teach the reader informative and helpful knowledge while due care should be taken by the user in the application of the information provided. The instructions and strategies are possibly not right for every reader and there is no guarantee that they work for everyone. Using this book and implementing the information/recipes therein contained is explicitly your own responsibility and risk. This work with all its contents, does not guarantee correctness, completion, quality or correctness of the provided information. Misinformation or misprints cannot be completely eliminated.

Printed in Great Britain
by Amazon

20812903R00064